Keep Track *of* Those Bills

Monthly Payment Journal

Activinotes

I0110553

Activinotes

DAILY JOURNALS, PLANNERS, NOTEBOOKS AND OTHER BLANK BOOKS

Name: ....

Address:..

E-mail : ....

Contact no's : ....

....

Net Income: ....

Remaining Bal: ....

Sunday	Monday	Tuesday	Wednesday

JANUARY

Thursday	Friday	Saturday	NOTES

BILL	AMOUNT	BALANCE	DUE

BILL	AMOUNT	BALANCE	DUE

BILL	AMOUNT	BALANCE	DUE

BILL	AMOUNT	BALANCE	DUE

Net Income: ....

Remaining Bal: ....

Sunday	Monday	Tuesday	Wednesday

FEBRUARY

Thursday	Friday	Saturday	NOTES

BILL	AMOUNT	BALANCE	DUE

BILL	AMOUNT	BALANCE	DUE

BILL	AMOUNT	BALANCE	DUE

BILL	AMOUNT	BALANCE	DUE

Net Income: ....

Remaining Bal: ....

Sunday	Monday	Tuesday	Wednesday

MARCH

Thursday	Friday	Saturday	NOTES

BILL	AMOUNT	BALANCE	DUE

BILL	AMOUNT	BALANCE	DUE

BILL	AMOUNT	BALANCE	DUE

BILL	AMOUNT	BALANCE	DUE

Net Income: ....

Remaining Bal: ....

Sunday	Monday	Tuesday	Wednesday

APRIL

Thursday	Friday	Saturday	NOTES

BILL	AMOUNT	BALANCE	DUE

BILL	AMOUNT	BALANCE	DUE

BILL	AMOUNT	BALANCE	DUE

BILL	AMOUNT	BALANCE	DUE

Net Income: ....

Remaining Bal: ....

Sunday	Monday	Tuesday	Wednesday

MAY

Thursday	Friday	Saturday	NOTES

BILL	AMOUNT	BALANCE	DUE

BILL	AMOUNT	BALANCE	DUE

BILL	AMOUNT	BALANCE	DUE

BILL	AMOUNT	BALANCE	DUE

Net Income: ....

Remaining Bal: ....

Sunday	Monday	Tuesday	Wednesday

JUNE

Thursday	Friday	Saturday	NOTES

BILL	AMOUNT	BALANCE	DUE

BILL	AMOUNT	BALANCE	DUE

BILL	AMOUNT	BALANCE	DUE

BILL	AMOUNT	BALANCE	DUE

Net Income: ....

Remaining Bal: ....

Sunday	Monday	Tuesday	Wednesday

Thursday	Friday	Saturday	NOTES

BILL	AMOUNT	BALANCE	DUE

BILL	AMOUNT	BALANCE	DUE

BILL	AMOUNT	BALANCE	DUE

BILL	AMOUNT	BALANCE	DUE

Net Income: ....

Remaining Bal: ....

Sunday	Monday	Tuesday	Wednesday

AUGUST

Thursday	Friday	Saturday	NOTES

BILL	AMOUNT	BALANCE	DUE

BILL	AMOUNT	BALANCE	DUE

BILL	AMOUNT	BALANCE	DUE

BILL	AMOUNT	BALANCE	DUE

Net Income: ....

Remaining Bal: ....

Sunday	Monday	Tuesday	Wednesday

SEPTEMBER

Thursday	Friday	Saturday	NOTES

BILL	AMOUNT	BALANCE	DUE

BILL	AMOUNT	BALANCE	DUE

BILL	AMOUNT	BALANCE	DUE

BILL	AMOUNT	BALANCE	DUE

Net Income: ....

Remaining Bal: ....

Sunday	Monday	Tuesday	Wednesday

OCTOBER

Thursday	Friday	Saturday	NOTES

BILL	AMOUNT	BALANCE	DUE

BILL	AMOUNT	BALANCE	DUE

BILL	AMOUNT	BALANCE	DUE

BILL	AMOUNT	BALANCE	DUE

Net Income: ....

Remaining Bal: ....

Sunday	Monday	Tuesday	Wednesday

NOVEMBER

Thursday	Friday	Saturday	NOTES

BILL	AMOUNT	BALANCE	DUE

BILL	AMOUNT	BALANCE	DUE

BILL	AMOUNT	BALANCE	DUE

BILL	AMOUNT	BALANCE	DUE

Net Income: ....

Remaining Bal: ....

Sunday	Monday	Tuesday	Wednesday

DECCEMBER

Thursday	Friday	Saturday	NOTES

BILL	AMOUNT	BALANCE	DUE

BILL	AMOUNT	BALANCE	DUE

BILL	AMOUNT	BALANCE	DUE

BILL	AMOUNT	BALANCE	DUE

www.ingramcontent.com/pod-product-compliance
Lightning Source LLC
Chambersburg PA
CBHW081334090426
42737CB00017B/3144
* 9 7 8 1 6 8 3 2 1 8 4 6 3 *